JOURI

RECOVERY

A Brain Injury Guide for Families

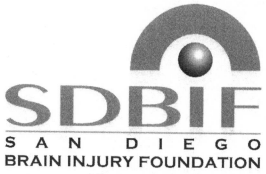

S A N   D I E G O
BRAIN INJURY FOUNDATION
Resources for the journey towards recovery

Bʏ ᴛʜᴇ San Diego Brain Injury Foundation

*Serving brain-injury survivors and their families
since 1983*

www.sdbif.org

Special thanks to

COUNTRY FRIENDS

The ideas, procedures, and suggestions in this book are not intended as a substitute for the medical advice of a trained health professional. All matters regarding your health require medical supervision. Consult your physician before adopting the suggestions in this book, as well as about any condition that may require medical attention. The author and publisher disclaim any liability arising directly or indirectly from the use of the book (or of any products mentioned herein).

Journey to Recovery: A brain injury guide for families is available for educational or special event use. For more information about discounted pricing for your organization or event, please contact info@sdbif.org

JOURNEY TO RECOVERY

A Brain Injury Guide for Families

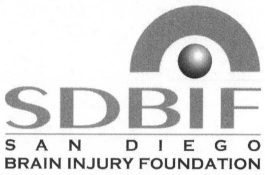

SDBIF

S A N   D I E G O
BRAIN INJURY FOUNDATION

Resources for the journey towards recovery

BY THE San Diego Brain Injury Foundation

*Serving brain-injury survivors and their families
since 1983*

*Originally Written by Jamie Reiter, Ph.D.
Updated and Revised by:
Teresa Dwight, M.S, CCC-SLP
Heike Kessler-Heiberg, M.A., CCC-SLP
Kathleen Munroe, M.S., CCC-SLP
Cynthia Pahr, M. Ed, CBIST
Ben Coughlan, J.D.
Ruth Curran, M.S.*

Cover photograph by Sylvia Prewo

DEDICATION

*To courageous survivors, dedicated medical
professionals, and generous caregivers.*

TABLE OF CONTENTS

INTRODUCTION

JOURNEY TO RECOVERY

---

*"Recovery unfolds like the dawn,
spreading glory on darkness, teasing
hope from despair."*

- C.H., Brain-injury Survivor

INTRODUCTION

This guide has been written for anyone who has been touched by brain injury; whether mild or severe, family or friend. This guide's goal is to provide survivors, caregivers and loved ones with the fundamental tools they need to travel the incredible journey of recovery. This guide is not meant to be read in one sitting. We hope you will find the information you need when you need it.

People like you—including brain-injury survivors, families of survivors, caregivers and medical experts—have provided useful information in the development of this guide. The guide has been designed to assist you from the moment you hear the "news" through all the stages of recovery. We hope this guide will condense information usually found in pamphlets, leaflets, websites and books into one easily searchable guidebook.

We also want to help you with issues that can arise after survivors are considered "recovered" by their doctors. The survivor may still struggle with a new way of life, a new sense of identity, changed relationships, job placement, driving, daily tasks, and emotions. These issues can affect caregivers and loved ones as well.

One of the most significant factors contributing to a survivor's recovery from brain injury is the involvement and support by the family. Though difficult, the journey can bring families together and help us appreciate what's important in life. Survivors not only need to receive support from their caregivers and loved ones, but also *they* need to support others as a contributing member of their community. This reciprocal relationship will serve to strengthen the resolve of anyone touched by brain injury.

WHAT HAPPENED?

CHAPTER ONE: WHAT HAPPENED?

The Crisis Begins

It starts out as an average day. You are at home doing laundry, in the car running errands, or at work. The phone rings, you answer it, and the voice on the other end says something, but the words don't register. You ask the person to repeat it.

"There has been an accident," the voice says.

Adding, "Are you the wife of Frank Smith?"

You say, "Yes."

"Frank has been in a car accident and we need you to come to the hospital right away."

This statement takes your breath away. Is this real? You go on autopilot and get in the car, driving in a daze the whole way. Thoughts race through your head, "Is he alive?"

1

"What condition will he be in?" "How am I going to handle this?"

After what seems like an eternity, you arrive at the waiting area at the hospital emergency room. No one can tell you anything except that there was a bad accident and Frank is in emergency surgery. After a while, the surgeon approaches you and says that it doesn't look good. "Frank has sustained a severe injury to the head. If he survives, he may not be able to speak or walk," the doctor says.

Your mind repeats that sentence again and again, but the meaning doesn't register.

What You May Be Feeling

Perhaps at this point, you start to panic. You feel as if your whole world is collapsing around you. No one has prepared you for this. Your feelings go from panic to fear to anger to confusion and back again. The doctors are taking good care of Frank, but you feel so helpless. All you can do is wait and pray.

After a night of little sleep, you start to face reality. You begin thinking of the possibilities:

Frank may not survive;
He survives, but is in a coma;
He's not in a coma, but he is paralyzed and can't speak;
He is not paralyzed, but he can't function the way he used to.

The list goes on and on. You imagine how this situation will affect your family. Frank will no longer be able to support you financially or emotionally. In fact, you may

2

have to support him. In addition to the emotions you felt yesterday, you now feel overwhelmed, stressed and devastated.

Questions swirl about you:

Where can I go for help?

Who should I contact?

What steps do I follow to take care of Frank and myself?

The following chapters will try to answer these questions. What you need to know is that these emotions are completely normal. You may even experience some that are not listed here.

CHAPTER TWO: FIRST STEPS

As you struggle to understand your loved one's injury, three steps are especially important:

1. Designate a family spokesperson;

*2. Identify medical team members
and their roles;*

3. Gather information.

Designate a Family Spokesperson

Being the spouse or closest kin of a brain-injury survivor does not necessarily mean you will be the best spokesperson for the family. The role of spokesperson is important because they are responsible for relaying information between the medical team and the family and should be the main contact whenever information needs to be communicated. The information needs to be explained promptly and accurately. This may involve making several phone calls a day. Emotions, work pressures, and other stresses may make it difficult for some family members to assume this role. Whether it is you or another family member, make sure that person has the motivation and availability to perform the task.

Identify Medical Team Members and Their Roles

You will meet several members of the survivor's medical team, all of whom have important roles. Be sure to write down the names and phone numbers of every member on the team. Your team may include some or all of the following:

Emergency Physician: Provides immediate care when patient is brought to the emergency room; will coordinate emergency care until hand-off to attending physician.

Attending Physician: Functions in the primary role.

Neurosurgeon: Coordinates medical treatment of the patient, deciding whether surgery is necessary and performing surgery when needed.

Neurologist: Specializes in problems in the nervous system; may help coordinate neurological care, medications, and testing. Neurologists may also coordinate neurological rehabilitation and management of neurological issues over the near and long term.

Anesthesiologist: Monitors the patient's anesthesia during surgery.

Plastic Surgeon: Reconstructs damaged skin and supporting tissues.

Physiatrist: Specializes in physical medicine and rehabilitation, often responsible for coordinating medical treatment.

Primary Nurse: Provides and coordinates patient care, serves as a liaison to the medical team, and is often a patient advocate. Nurses are very knowledgeable and good resources for information.

Respiratory Therapist: Ensures that the patient can breathe adequately.

Physical Therapist: Helps the patient regain gross motor movement including sitting, walking etc.

Occupational Therapist: Helps with activities of daily living (i.e., bathing, dressing, brushing teeth) and fine motor skills such as writing and using cooking utensils.

Speech-Language Pathologist: Helps the patient with communication (including speaking, comprehension, reading and writing), cognition (including memory) and swallowing function, in addition to providing alternative forms of communication when necessary.

Audiologist: Provides comprehensive hearing testing and treatment services as needed.

Social Worker: Assists patients and families with social, emotional or financial problems resulting from the injury.

Nutritionist: Consults with the patient and family about eating habits that would most benefit the patient.

Neuropsychologist: Evaluates and treats behaviors related to brain function, including determining degree of impairment compared to pre-injury functioning.

Psychologist: Gives supportive counseling to patients and their families to address specific problems they have relating to the injury.

Recreational Therapist and Child Life Specialist: Provides treatment through recreational and leisure activities to promote the independent physical, cognitive, and social-emotional abilities by enhancing current skills and facilitating the establishment of new skills

Special Education Teacher: Evaluates the academic achievement levels of children and adolescents in order to assist in educational planning.

Gather Information

With all of the commotion and confusion surrounding a brain injury, you will want to gather as much relevant information as possible and keep that information organized and accessible. A good person to keep this information is the designated family spokesperson. The information can be overwhelming – having one person to collect and coordinate the incoming and outgoing information can be vital. Some items to gather are: information related to the survivor's actual injury, medical history, medications, hospitalizations, insurance records, legal and financial information, and a journal of questions, answers, and concerns. By gathering information in an organized manner, you will begin to reclaim some feeling of control in your life.

CHAPTER THREE: GETTING INFORMED

Learning about Brain Injury

During this stressful time, family members and loved ones may feel confused about what's going on. Learning as much as possible about brain-injury will help you feel more in control and help other family members to understand what is going on. By getting involved, you also create a support system for the brain injured individual. Do not be afraid to ask questions. The internet is a wonderful resource, as are libraries, local colleges and universities, community centers, government offices, hospitals and medical team members. This chapter should help direct you to many of those resources.

Your community may have an organization like the San Diego Brain Injury Foundation to guide you toward helpful information and find others who are also struggling with brain-injury issues.

11

For those who want to know more about the occurrence and nature of brain injuries, this chapter will provide you with relevant data.

Types of Brain Injury

"My injuries were serious. My jaw was broken in three places, all my teeth were lying in my mouth and my nose was gone. I have had a total of four major surgeries to reconstruct my face, complete with 48 screws and six metal plates in my mouth and jaw. I lost a fifth of my brain in that incident and was in a coma for three and a half months. I am proud to say that I have gotten some gross movements back in my left side and I can walk on my own."

- R. T., Brain-injury Survivor

Many people are confused about **traumatic** versus **non-traumatic brain injury**. Isn't all brain-injury "traumatic?" In medical terms, an injury that occurs from an external physical impact is traumatic; one with a biological origin, such as disease or heredity, is non-traumatic.

Traumatic brain-injury typically occurs as a result of an accident: motor vehicle, fall, bicycle, or sports-related. It also can occur as a result of intent: gunshot wound (self-inflicted or by others), blast injuries or other physical assault. **Non-traumatic brain injury** may result from strokes, aneurysms, tumors, degenerative neurological disorders, loss of oxygen, brain infections and other conditions.

Symptoms of Brain Injury

Whether traumatic or non-traumatic, brain injury can result in a variety of symptoms: some short-term, and others prolonged or permanent. It is important to remember that each individual will exhibit different symptoms (even some not mentioned below) and to varying degrees. No two brain injuries are the same, however different injuries can often be broken down into general categories of symptoms.

We will describe three categories of symptoms:

- Physical/Sensory
- Cognitive/Communicative
- Emotional/Behavioral

Physical and sensory symptoms are often those that are most obvious to survivors and their loved ones. Treatment is typically straightforward. Common examples include:

- Fatigue
- Seizures
- Loss of motor control and coordination
- Spasticity (increased muscle tone)

Sensory sensitivity (e.g., noise sensitivity, visual misperceptions, blurred vision, double vision)

- Difficulty with speech production
- Headaches
- Dizziness
- Bladder and bowel incontinence
- Nausea and vomiting
- Difficulty sleeping

- Balance difficulties
- Loss of smell/taste/hearing
- Temperature regulation

Cognitive and communicative symptoms can be a source of great frustration both for the survivor and caregivers. These symptoms are related to intellect, language, memory, attention, mental organization, and non-verbal communication (Examples: body language, facial expressions). Common examples include:

- Loss of short-term or long-term memory
- Difficulty concentrating
- Confusion
- Slowed thinking
- Reduced organizational skills
- Poor planning and problem solving
- Difficulty handling more than one thing at a time
- Difficulty completing tasks or staying on topic
- Impaired judgment or reasoning
- Less flexibility
- Short attention span
- Lack of initiative
- Impairments of perception
- Impaired communication skills for verbalizing their thoughts and understanding what they hear
- Talks a lot more or less than used to
- Reading and writing difficulties

Emotional and behavioral symptoms also require a great deal of patience and understanding from the survivor's loved ones. These symptoms can be a direct consequence of the brain injury or develop as a result of their emotional struggle dealing with impairments. Emotional/behavioral symptoms include:

- Aggression
- Mood swings
- Anxiety, depression and/or withdrawal
- Loss of interest in activities
- Impulsive behavior
- Lack of sexual inhibition
- Restlessness
- Increased frustration
- Denial
- Self-centeredness
- Lowered self-esteem
- Difficulty controlling emotions
- Lack of motivation

Any of these symptoms can affect other symptoms. Even mild symptoms can interfere with a person's ability to function effectively at work, in personal relationships, and in daily life. These symptoms can also have a profound effect on a person's self-confidence and self-esteem.

Incidence, Prevalence, Demographics

Brain injury does not discriminate. According to the Centers for Disease Control and Prevention (CDC), estimates of the number of people who have survived a TBI is broad—brain injury may go unreported—and ranges from 2.5 to 6.5 million of varying ages and backgrounds. Although these figures can be discouraging, they may also help caregivers realize that they are not alone. (http://www.cdc.gov/traumaticbraininjury/get_the_facts.html)

How the Brain Works

For many brain-injury survivors and their loved ones, it may be helpful to learn about the areas of the brain that have been damaged, and what can happen as a result of the damage. Although a great deal is known about brain function, there is still much more to be learned.

In healthy individuals, the brain is composed of neurons (nerve cells), which are essentially communication fibers. Neurons carry messages throughout the brain and body, and the brain uses these messages to perform various functions, including moving, breathing, thinking, speaking, sensing, emotion, and most of the things our bodies can do. The brain is protected by cerebrospinal fluid, three linings (meninges) and the skull.

The brain itself is divided into left and right hemispheres. Within each hemisphere are four sections, or lobes: frontal, occipital, parietal, and temporal; which make up the cerebrum. The limbic system, made up of the thalamus, hypothalamus, amygdala and the hippocampus, is located right under the cerebrum. Toward the base of the brain are the cerebellum and brain stem. Each section of the brain has certain functions associated with it, as described.

Frontal lobe

Planning/Anticipation
Mental flexibility
Problem solving
Initiation
Judgment
Self-awareness

Attention/Concentration
Personality/Emotion
Inhibition of behavior
Self-Monitoring
Speaking
Organization

Occipital Lobe

Vision
Visual perception
Identification of
    shapes, sizes, and colors

Parietal Lobe

Spatial perception
Sense of touch

Temporal Lobe

Organization sequencing
Language comprehension

Memory
Hearing

Cerebellum

Skilled motor activity
Balance

Coordination

Brain Stem

Heart rate
Arousal and consciousness

Breathing
Sleep and wake cycles

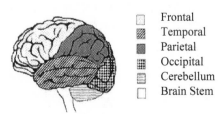

Frontal
Temporal
Parietal
Occipital
Cerebellum
Brain Stem

17

Injury to any of these areas can interfere with the functions mentioned above. Symptoms can vary depending upon the individual, how severe the injury was, and even which hemisphere was involved. In general, injuries to the left side of the brain can affect movement of the right half of the body, language difficulties, depression, and impaired logic. Injury to the right hemisphere can result in difficulty moving the left side of the body, visual-spatial problems, changes in creativity, and decreased awareness of defects.

Limbic System

Fight or flight reaction
Emotions
Putting together of recent memory
Regulation of appetite, temperature, sex drive, etc.

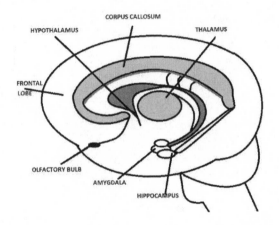

Injuries to the limbic system may help explain some difficulties with memory, emotional regulation, and the ability to filter what is happening in the surroundings. Many traumatic injuries involve jostling of the brain inside the skull which may result in injuries to other areas of the brain in addition to the area of impact. Injuries due to lack

18

of oxygen or illness may result in more widespread damage effecting many areas of the brain.

Classification and Levels of Brain Injury

Brain injury can be viewed along a continuum that incorporates concussion, mild brain injury, moderate brain injury and severe brain injury. However, as we learn more about the brain, and more about brain injuries, classifications, testing and treatment will continue to change. Each type of brain injury varies depending upon: (1) absence/presence of loss of consciousness; (2) length of unconsciousness (3) length of amnesia; (4) resulting cognitive, behavioral and physical problems; and (5) recovery.

Concussion & Mild Traumatic Brain Injury (mTBI)

The topic of concussions and mild Traumatic Brain Injury (mTBI) has gained interest in the community as a result of increased news coverage and reports about soldiers and blast injuries, brain safety in children's sports and professional sports; and the release of the movie, *Concussion,* about chronic traumatic encephalopathy. Searching for information about mTBI and concussion can be confusing. The opinions on how to classify the injury fall in one of two camps: those who consider them synonymous and those who consider them overlapping but not synonymous. In both cases, the brain injury is the result of a direct hit or jolt to the head. The brain bounces back and forth in the skull damaging the underlying cells and their connections. The matter to keep in mind is that mTBI and concussion are brain injuries and should be taken seriously.

The Brain Injury Association estimates that "approximately 75% of all brain injuries fall in the "concussion-mTBI continuum." Specialists who work in the field of brain injury recognize the need to continue refining the definitions and terminology along this end of the brain injury severity continuum. While a difficult task, it will assist the public, and the medical community that serves them, in making decisions about when to seek treatment and what type of treatment to seek.

GETTING INFORMED

The Road to Rehabilitation Series, Part 8: Journey Toward Understanding: Concussion & Mild Brain Injury description is summarized below.

Concussion Grade 1	Concussion Grade 2	Concussion Grade 3
Confused but remains conscious.	Conscious, but develops amnesia.	Loses consciousness for seconds or minutes. *mTBI has a loss of consciousness of no more than 30 minutes*
SIGNS: Temporarily confused, dazed, unable to think clearly, has trouble following directions.	SIGNS: Similar to Grade 1.	SIGNS: Noticeable disruption of brain function exhibited in physical, cognitive and behavioral ways.
TIME: Symptoms clear within 15 minutes.	TIME: Symptoms last more than 15 minutes.	TIME: Symptoms may last for extended periods. *mTBI includes post traumatic amnesia (a period immediately after the injury where the person is not able to recall information) of no more than 24 minutes. And an initial Glasgow Coma Scale of 13-15 after 30 minutes.*

The important "take-aways" in this discussion are that the symptoms overlap, the term "mild" can be a misnomer, and seeking appropriate help is paramount.

Signs and Symptoms that an Injured Person Can Experience

Because the accurate diagnosis is challenging especially in cases where there is no documented or observed loss of consciousness, it is important to look at not just the injury itself but also the resulting symptoms and changes in behaviors.

- Dizziness
- Headaches
- Blurred vision/other visual disturbances/sensitivity to light
- Nausea/vomiting
- Fatigue
- Seizures
- Sensitivity to light/sound/ringing in the ears/hearing changes
- Sleeping challenges (falling asleep, staying asleep, sleeping soundly enough, not feeling rested after sleep)
- Cognitive challenges (attention & concentration/learning new information/keeping up with conversations/reaction times, impulsivity, reading & understanding what is heard in conversation)
- Emotional challenges (depression, anxiety, irritability, crying easily)

22

The Misnomer of "mild"

The word "mild" in the context of an mTBI only refers to the **severity of the initial injury—it is not immediately life threatening.** It does not consider how severely the injury potentially effects a person's ability to meet the demands of day to day life; nor how permanent these effects are. In many cases, as the physical symptoms are in the process of resolving, the injured person or those close to them begin to notice differences from their previous self.

Seeking Help & Moving Forward

Seeking help is not limited to when a person is first injured when the need can be more apparent—they've hit their head and are vomiting, complaining of severe headaches, having a hard time staying awake, or going in and out of consciousness. Moving forward, recognize that symptoms can be present months after the original injury. Seeking help when symptoms are present, regardless of when they are observed or experienced, is most important.

Other precautions to keep in mind include:

- Protect your head —wear a helmet.
- Avoid activities that could cause re-injury to both your head and brain.
- Follow your doctor's orders—i.e., when to return to work/school, medications, driving, drinking alcohol.
- Give yourself time to heal.

- Rest your brain—minimize use of electronics and other things that can overstimulate you.
- Follow the new guidelines for return to play that are in the works. These new guidelines include baseline testing, safer playing techniques, recommendations for removal from play, and new protective gear technology.

Tools to Describe a Brain Injury

Your medical team will use different measures to describe the brain injury. Two of the more common scales are the Glasgow Coma Scale and the Rancho Los Amigos Scale.

Glasgow Coma Scale

The Glasgow Coma Scale is often used at the scene of an accident or at the emergency room and measures the level of consciousness through three main responses: eye opening, best motor response, and best verbal response. These are graded using the numerical system below. The lower the score, the more severe the injury. This scale does not always accurately predict how well a person will recover or regain their functioning, nor is it sensitive to cognitive or psychological changes after mild traumatic injuries (concussions). It is also important to understand, however, a perfect, or near perfect, score on a Glasgow Coma Scale test does not mean a person has not suffered a brain injury.

GETTING INFORMED

Response	Score
Eye Opening	
Spontaneous	1
To speech	3
To pain	2
None	1
Best Motor Response	
Obeys commands	6
Localized movements	5
Withdraws	4
Abnormal bending and flexing	3
Involuntary straightening and extending	2
None	1
Best Verbal Response	
Is oriented	5
Confused conversation	4
Inappropriate words	3
Incomprehensible sounds	2
None	1

Mild: GCS 13-15
Moderate: GCS 9-12
Severe: GCS 3-8 (You cannot score lower than a 3.)

25

Rancho Los Amigos Scale

Originally developed as a test, the Rancho Los Amigos Scale is used to describe cognitive and behavioral functioning after a brain injury, and may be used repeatedly throughout the entire rehabilitation process to measure progress. The revised scale (Hagen, 1979) consists of ten levels, and is helpful for determining how an individual is progressing.

Level 1: *No Response.* The individual appears to be in a deep sleep or coma, does not respond to any stimulus, including voices, sounds, light or touch.

Level 2: *Generalized Response.* The individual remains primarily asleep, but may respond to certain stimuli such as pain. Movements do not seem to have any purpose. Eyes may open but do not focus on anything in particular.

Level 3: *Localized Response.* The individual remains alert for several minutes at a time and responds more consistently to general stimuli such as turning the head to noise, looking at people, or squeezing a hand when asked.

Level 4: *Confused and Agitated.* The individual is confused and agitated about where he or she is and what is happening around him or her. The slightest provocation can lead to aggression, restlessness, or verbal abuse. Conversations may be confused or coherent.

Level 5: *Confused, Inappropriate, Non-agitated.* The individual is confused and may not make sense in conversations. Can follow simple directions.

Agitation is no longer a major issue, although the individual may experience some frustration as memory begins to return.

Level 6: *Confused, Appropriate.* The individual's speech makes sense and he or she can perform simple tasks such as getting dressed, eating, and brushing teeth. Knowing when to start and stop an activity may be difficult, as well as learning new things.

Level 7: *Automatic, Appropriate.* If physically able, the individual is able to perform all self-care activities and can carry out routine activities. Is coherent. He or she may have trouble remembering recent events and discussions. Supervision is needed for safety. Judgment and problem-solving abilities continue to be impaired, but there is poor awareness that they exist.

Level 8: *Purposeful, Appropriate, Stand by assistance.* The individual is independent for familiar tasks, with distractions, for about an hour; and can process new information. Judgment and problem-solving abilities are improved to allow acknowledgement of impairments but is not able to "catch" problems when they happen. With the increase in insight can be signs of depression, irritability and low frustration tolerance.

Level 9: *Purposeful, Appropriate, Stand by assistance **on request**.* The individual is able to shift between tasks for about two hours. Able to identify how cognitive problems interfere with a task after the fact but benefits from assistance to identify potential problems and adjust to day-to-day demands. Needs to be monitored for emotional and/or behavioral issues.

Level 10: *Purposeful, Appropriate, Modified Independent.* The individual is goal directed and able to manage multiple tasks but may need planned breaks. Benefits from systems, strategies and additional time to participate in usual activities.

As patients improve after a brain injury, they typically will move from one level to the next. It is common for an individual to experience symptoms in more than one level at one time. There is no set time period for remaining at one level or another—each individual will progress differently.

Treatment and Rehabilitation

Depending upon the severity and location of the brain injury, the patient may spend time in any of several types of care units, undergo several forms of diagnosis and treatment, and receive various kinds of long-term or follow-up care. After the initial visit to the emergency room, some patients will be admitted to the hospital, followed by treatment in a skilled nursing facility, nursing home, or in the patient's own home. Many types of equipment and procedures will be used at each stage of recovery, and the length of recovery will vary.

The Hospital Stay

A patient with moderate to severe brain injury can expect to spend several weeks to months in the hospital.

There are two main units in the hospital that provide comprehensive care for the brain-injury patient: the intensive care unit and acute care. The medical team in each unit will continue to evaluate, monitor, and treat the patient.

Intensive Care Unit (ICU): This is an inpatient unit where patients with moderate to severe injuries are taken following the emergency room. The goals of the ICU are to stabilize the patient, manage his care, and prevent medical crises.

Acute Hospital Care: Once a patient is stabilized, he may be transferred to a regular hospital unit. Acute care is also inpatient and still provides essential care for the patient's well-being. The patient may receive care and treatment from members of the medical team such as the physiatrist, various therapists, rehabilitation nurses, neuropsychologists, and social workers.

"During the surgery that followed, complications set in resulting in aphasia, which essentially erased Don's prior ability to speak, read, write and do math. He knew what he wanted to say, but any words other than 'yes' and 'no' came out as gibberish. Even something as simple as the alphabet was no longer recognizable and had to be relearned during hours of intensive rehabilitation."

- Family Member

Rehabilitation

Following acute hospital care, patients will likely undergo extensive rehabilitation to regain everyday functioning. The types of rehabilitation required will depend upon the location and extent of the injury as well as on the individual patient's needs. Length of rehabilitation will also vary, from several weeks to several months, possibly even years.

Types of Therapies

Patients may undergo one or more of several types of therapies:

Physical therapy: Helps to regain physical movement and function.

Occupational therapy: Helps to regain fine motor skills.

Speech-Language therapy: Helps regain normal or alternate forms of communication. Typically includes strategies and exercises to work with memory and thinking processes. Also addresses swallowing disorders.

Cognitive rehabilitation: Addresses difficulties with memory, attention, planning, problem-solving, organization, behavior, and social communication.

Therapeutic Recreation: Helps to integrate skills learned in treatment settings into community settings using leisure and recreational activities.

Each of these types of therapies is performed or managed by the corresponding therapist, as described in Chapter Two.

Rehabilitation Settings

The types of rehabilitation described above may be performed in a variety of settings. The location will depend upon the needs of the patient, the recommendations of the medical team, and, possibly, insurance coverage.

Acute Inpatient Rehabilitation: Focuses on intensive cognitive and physical therapies in the early months after injury. May be based in the hospital, off-site, or in specialized skilled care facilities. Typically for individuals who are able to tolerate a minimum of three hours of therapy.

Sub-acute Rehabilitation: Often performed in a skilled nursing facility or nursing home, and focuses on less intensive rehabilitation, traditionally over a longer period of time.

Post-Acute Rehabilitation Options: Therapy options after the hospital stay.

Home Health: Therapy and nursing services are delivered in the home under the condition that the patient is home bound and is not able to receive services outside of the home.

Outpatient Therapy: Typically for patients who do not require inpatient treatment. May include those who have progressed but need assistance with more complex tasks or those whose impairments are not severe enough to require inpatient treatment. May take place in the hospital, skilled nursing facility, or other settings.

Day Rehabilitation (Day Hospital, Day Treatment): Takes place in the hospital or off-site facility as a structured program; the patient returns home at night.

Community Re-entry Programs: Designed to assist the patient regain skills needed to return to more independent living and meaningful activities (examples: hobbies, volunteering, or work), while the survivor typically lives at "home". Therapies focus on higher level motor, cognitive, and social skills, and can take place in the home, community or in a rehabilitation center.

School Re-entry Plans: For school-aged children, special education Individual Education Plan (IEP) or a Section 504 Plan (described in Chapter 9) may be developed. These can provide services and accommodations to aid school re-entry and provide school therapies and educational support.

Transitional Living Centers: Provide housing for brain-injury survivors, with the goal of helping individuals attain independent living. Programs may vary in levels of assistance, depending upon the needs of the individual.

"I had two good words. I could finally say 'cat' and 'dog'."

- D. S., Brain-injury Survivor

Selecting a Rehabilitation Program

As with any form of treatment, it is essential that family members research different hospitals, rehabilitation programs, treatment centers, and personnel. A facility or program that helps one survivor may not be as helpful to another individual. In addition, once a program or facility has been selected, family members should continually monitor treatment and progress to ensure that the appropriate treatment is being received. Many communities offer assistance in providing care, as well as helping family members locate qualified specialists.

Some of the questions family members should ask when selecting a rehabilitation program are:

- Does the program specialize in brain injury?

- Does the program address the patient's and family's needs?
- Does the program offer a continuum of rehab programs/services to address the needs of the brain injured over time?
- Can they give you good references or referrals from patients who have gone through the program?
- What does the program cost? Is it covered by insurance?
- Can family members observe the program?
- How are family, friends, and caregivers involved with the program?
- Are there support groups for the family?
- Are the facility and staff members licensed, and if so, by whom?
- Is the program accredited by an internationally recognized organization?
- What other accreditation does the program have?
- What is the staff turnover rate? (If the staff is continually changing, that may indicate problems with the facility.)
- Can changes to the program be made if requested by a family member and if it is in the interest of the patient? What is the process for making changes?
- Is the facility clean and pleasant?
- Is the staff professional and friendly? Do they seem to care about the patients?
- What is the procedure for discharging the patient?

There are many questions family members can and should be asking when considering a rehabilitation facility, and the list above should not be considered comprehensive.

Your local hospital and community health centers should be able to provide you with a list of rehabilitation providers. Information can also be obtained on the Internet or through national health organizations.

How to Make Things Easier for Everyone

There are some things caregivers and family members can do to minimize stress on everyone: the patient, other family members, the medical team, and yourself.

- If the patient is in the confused and agitated state, minimize his stimulation. This includes limiting flowers, television, visitors, phone calls, and even physical contact. In fact, a gentle touch can be extremely agitating to a patient in this state. Speak in a calm, slow manner and in simple sentences.
- Do not talk down to the patient.
- Limit visits to the morning hours, when the patient may have the most energy. This applies to after the patient returns home, as well.
- Encourage visitors to briefly ask the patient how he or she is doing, then to move onto other topics of conversation. Make a strong effort NOT to ask a lot of questions. Use simple yes/no questions and/or provide simple choices. Allow time for a response.
- Let the medical team do their job. You may know the patient, but they know brain injury. You can do your research, make suggestions, and ask questions. Actually, we encourage that you do so. Just realize that your medical team is doing their best for the patient.
- Follow their recommendations and adhere to hospital rules.

- Ask each member of the medical team how and when they prefer to be contacted should you have a question.

- Ask who to contact in an emergency or if you have a question that can't wait.

- Write down all of your questions and the answers you are given.

- Keeping a detailed "medical notebook" with records of medical procedures and contacts, questions and answers, etc. can be very helpful in becoming a good advocate for your loved one.

- Try to realize that members of your medical team are human and have their own pressures and concerns. A little morale booster goes a long way—send flowers, write a thank you note, or just smile and tell them you appreciate what they are doing.

Take care of yourself! See Chapter Five for ideas on coping. If people offer to help, let them. It will not only relieve some of the burden on you, but it also will let others feel useful. Feel free to ask others to help, as well. Talk to friends, family, social workers, and other professionals about what you are going through. Join support groups and keep yourself occupied.

CHAPTER FOUR:
THE PATIENT'S EMOTIONAL JOURNEY

---

*"We act sweet, we pick up after ourselves, we
get to [survivor group] class on time...you'd
think everything is wonderful and good! But
it's NOT! I can't do what I used to do—I
can't even be how I used to be. The one thing
I've been scared of is that this new life would
be empty, hard and meaningless. The one
thing I don't want to say—and I'm scared I'll
mean it someday— is that I'm sorry or mad
that they saved me."*

-C.H., Brain-injury Survivor

What the Survivor May Be Feeling

Many brain injury survivors feel a loss of identity. Many
of us take for granted the things with which we identify
ourselves: our job, our hobbies, our relationships and roles.
Imagine all of a sudden not being able to go to work, drive a

37

car, cook a meal, play a game of basketball, help your children with their homework, console a friend, go for a walk, or even hug your family. For brain injury survivors the loss of ability to accomplish day-to-day tasks that many of us take for granted becomes particularly difficult. Survivors often must learn to accept assistance from others for even the most basic skills. They must come to terms with their new limitations, new roles, new sense of who they are, and where they fit in. The person they (and you) knew before the injury has been replaced by someone who is, in essence, a stranger. This can be more difficult to deal with than the physical limitations.

Many times, an individual who has suffered a brain injury will experience feelings that others would consider natural, such as frustration, disappointment and depression. However, injured individuals may also experience feelings that come as a surprise for family members and loved ones. Along with the brain injury comes a whole new set of circumstances. Without the ability to care for themselves, they may begin to feel useless and helpless. Having to rely on someone else to take care of one's basic needs can make them feel like a burden, no matter how good the caregiver is at assuring them that they are not.

One of the issues that brain-injury survivors frequently encounter is that they do not appear physically disabled. In fact, their disability may be solely cognitive in nature; that's why brain injury is often called the "hidden disability." Without the physical reminders, others may not be aware of the patient's limitations and can act intolerant, causing the brain injury survivor further embarrassment and frustration.

They may or may not express these feelings. Putting yourself in their shoes, and putting aside your own issues and wants, will help you really understand what they need. It is not only the survivor that will need to come to grips with a new identity, but their loved ones will have to accept this new identity as well.

What the Survivor Needs From Family and Friends

Every brain-injured individual is different. It may take some trial-and-error to figure out what they need. This may take some time and cause temporary uneasiness when mistakes are made, but by learning what they need, you can help speed up recovery. Based on comments from other brain-injury survivors, we have compiled a list of some of the qualities they found most helpful from their caregivers and loved ones.

Patience: It will likely be difficult for survivors to re-learn tasks, be able to hear what you are saying, remember the simplest things and follow the proper way to behave. Muster all of your strength to avoid pushing them, getting annoyed, or doing things for them that they can do for themselves.

Respect: Keep in mind that a person with a brain injury is still a human being and deserves respect. For example, if a person is unable to communicate, we may assume that they do not understand what is going on around them. Someone who cannot speak may be perfectly able to hear and understand language. Speak to the adult survivor as an adult and treat them as an adult. In the presence of others, show respect for them. Share in their joy and accomplishments, no matter how small they may seem to you.

Understanding: In order to practice patience and respect, caregivers and loved ones need to adopt a well-informed perspective. This means not only learning about brain-injury and its consequences, but also being able to show the survivor and others that you are aware of and empathize with their situation. They do not want your pity but rather an acceptance of who they are, even with their limitations and abilities.

Knowing When and When NOT to Push: This can be very tricky. Different survivors will respond to different types of encouragement to recover their abilities. Use them as your guide. Begin by gradually encouraging the survivor. At each step of the way, either ask them how they are doing or observe their behavior and facial expressions to determine if you need to back off. The goal is to help them try to the best of their ability while minimizing the frustration that accompanies the effort. You can acknowledge how difficult this process is and give them positive feedback.

Flexibility: You have figured out the right way to encourage the survivor. Even if one day you unwittingly upset them you may have done nothing different than before. Brain-injury survivors can experience mood changes. What worked once may not work another time. The range of emotions and challenges the patient experiences changes throughout the recovery process. You may need to change your routine or how you behave.

Sense of Humor: Many people in the company of a brain-injury survivor are so afraid to offend the survivor that they clam up or act stiff and distant. Remember that brain-injury survivors spend much of their time "surrounded" by their injury. Sometimes, lighten the seriousness of the moment by saying or doing something to make them laugh. Naturally, you won't make jokes about their limitations. Bring a joke book, a cassette or video of their favorite comedian. You may still offend someone, but that's the chance many comedians take! Feel free to laugh if they make a joke!

Love: This goes without saying. If you are having trouble expressing your love for the survivor, try visualizing the times in your life where you felt the most love for them and try to regain that moment. Think of things about the person that you used to love and that you love now. Imagine how good it will feel for them to feel loved. Along with laughter, love can do wonders for helping the survivor heal.

CHAPTER FIVE: COPING

"Whenever someone would ask how I was holding up, I would politely smile and say 'fine.' They knew, as well as I, that I wasn't fine. In fact, I was exhausted and felt like a raging volcano ready to erupt. It was when my 12-year-old daughter almost cowered at my asking her if she finished her homework that I realized I had been snapping at her relentlessly. Now I take better care of myself. I talk to a psychologist. I started bike riding with my daughter and I feel I can now be a better mother."

- J. P., Caregiver

Just as important as the brain injury survivor's well-being is the well-being of their support group. This includes family, friends and caregivers. It is easy for the loved ones to get engrossed in caring for that individual and putting their own needs and wants aside. What many people *don't* realize is that by not taking care of themselves, they are also hurting the survivor, and other loved ones. Think about what would happen if you burn out and weren't available for your injured loved one when you were really needed? As human beings we have the need to live our own lives and take care of ourselves to a reasonable extent.

The first step in learning to take care of yourself is learning how to cope with your feelings. Caring for a brain injury survivor is a new reality for YOU as well.

The next step in taking care of yourself is knowing what to expect from your new reality. If you expect someone with a broken leg to go for a run with you, you will only set yourself up for disappointment and frustration. Similarly, you cannot expect someone with a brain injury to function the way they used to, or even the way you think they ought to now. Part of knowing what to expect is learning not to expect anything other than one's best efforts. If a brain-injury survivor is taking months to utter one word, then perhaps that is the best they can do. If you are disappointed in yourself for not being with them seven days per week, give yourself a break—you are probably doing your best as well. When you don't have such expectations, you learn to appreciate and be happy with the little things.

The third step is learning to strike a balance between encouraging progress and accepting limitations. Look for support groups and other resources to help you create this balance.

Accepting and Managing Feelings

Many of the emotions you felt during the first few days may last for days, weeks, or even months. You may have moments of panic, fear, anger, confusion, frustration, stress, and feeling overwhelmed – that is normal. What is helpful to know is that, with time, most of these feelings will subside. It is important *not* to suppress your feelings or blame yourself for having them, or even wonder why it's taking so long for the feelings to go away.

One common emotion that family members experience is denial. They refuse to acknowledge that things are as bad as they are. They believe that they are handling things just fine, and that everything will be back to normal soon. Although this does not represent reality, it can be a healthy, short-term way for some people to cope. In a sense, denial gives those experiencing it a "vacation" from the constant turmoil they are feeling. In the same way an actual vacation can renew and refresh an individual, this sort of mental vacation can also prepare individuals for handling upcoming issues. Denial can be a problem, however, if it persists. Coming to grips with your new reality is a process, but it a vital process to helping your survivor, your family and yourself.

As a family member, you may experience tremendous feelings of guilt, and may either blame yourself or others for allowing them to do something that contributed to their injury. A certain amount of guilt is normal, but extreme guilt and/or blaming others can be damaging. Families need to keep things in perspective: don't dwell on the past but try to focus on the present.

There are things you can do to deal with your feelings appropriately. Instead of taking your anger out on yourself or someone else, utilize the many stress-reducing strategies as described later in this chapter.

What to Expect During the Recovery Process

"I was unable to drive for several years. After finally getting my license reinstated, my difficulties with direction and short-term memory made driving alone extremely difficult and frightening."

- D. S., Brain-injury Survivor

From the Patient/Survivor

The brain injury survivor is understandably going through a lot, both physically and emotionally. Each injury is different and each survivor is different. They can be a trooper and roll with the punches, or they can be devastated. There may be times when they are in denial, depressed, and not motivated to try to recover. There may be other times when they are so anxious to get better that they will put in all of their effort to attain the goal of recovery. There may be times when they need a shoulder to cry on, a coach to push them to recover, or merely to be left alone. Family and caregivers may at times serve as emotional "punching bags" for them. In fact, the brain injury survivor may feel so loved and reassured by certain family members that they feel safe enough to express feelings in this way. On the other hand, many will be surprisingly cheerful.

No matter how the survivor acts and reacts, they will need to know that family and friends are available for support. This includes encouraging them when appropriate, leaving them alone when asked, and making a joke or two to cheer them up. If a patient does take some anger out on family or friends, it is important that everyone not take it personally. Patience will become a new reality for loved ones of brain injury survivors.

From Yourself

Most family members and caregivers try to become superheroes. You may expect yourself to be available at the drop of a hat, to be encouraging, understanding, patient, supportive, and all of the other qualities your brain injury survivor needs. And you will have to accomplish all of this while maintaining a life of your own. It is important to recognize your limitations because over-exerting yourself is not healthy for them or yourself.

Caregivers can expect to experience the joys of seeing someone accomplish something they never thought they would accomplish. However, caregivers can also expect to lose their cool, to get impatient, to want to give up, to leave, and to break down. We are human—these things are going to happen. That is why it is so important for caregivers and those closely involved in the recovery process to take regular breaks.

Learning to Strike a Balance

"I was by his side 24 hours a day for two months. I got little sleep, ate poorly, and practically cut myself off from the rest of the world...It finally hit me when I suddenly panicked and had to get out of the hospital, right away. I drove for two hours, collected my thoughts, and found that for the past two months I had lost my identity, just as he had...I had become just one of the pieces of equipment in the hospital. During that drive I made the difficult decision that I had to limit my visits and make time for myself."

- C.R., Caregiver

There is an art to maintaining a balance between fulfilling your obligations to others while being true to yourself.

Taking Care of Yourself

Each person needs different things in order to feel taken care of. Some may need weekly massages, some may need a round of golf, some may need a shoulder to cry on, and some may want to go shopping. Whatever brings you the greatest sense of comfort (as long as it is not destructive), should be done on a regular basis. Turn off the ringer on your phone and have someone else (the family spokesperson) update family members on the survivor's condition. Assign different family members to different tasks and hospital shifts.

Strategies such as deep breathing, leaving the room, going for a walk, and squeezing a "stress" ball can help you deal with your emotions at that moment. Helping others should make you feel energized. If not, you need to take more breaks and do more for yourself.

It is often very helpful for family members to share their feelings with each other, with friends, other family members, or professionals. The important thing is to get them out! Speak with others who have gone through something similar. Join support groups. Encourage others to ask questions and to express their feelings as well. At minimum, keep a journal (written or on tape) to express everything you are feeling.

Your local hospitals and community centers can provide you with information on caregiving, and the Internet has several sites for caregiver support. We strongly suggest you contact these or other agencies and get involved in a support group.

Empower Yourself

The suggestions in this section can apply for both the caregiver and the patient. During stressful times such as this, many people feel a loss of control. Although it is not possible to control the person's brain injury, recovery, treatment, behavior, emotions, etc., it is possible to regain a sense of control simply by taking initiative for the things that *are* in your control. This may include doing things to improve your health and well-being, helping others, and making life simpler for yourself.

Exercise

There are few health experts, if any, who would argue that an otherwise healthy individual shouldn't exercise. Under a physician's guidance, exercise can alleviate stress, improve your health, help your self-esteem, and give you a sense that you are accomplishing something positive. The latter benefit may be most relevant for caregivers who are feeling helpless.

Volunteer Your Time

There is probably nothing more valuable than helping others without expecting anything in return. If for whatever reason you cannot help your loved one to the extent that you desire, you can volunteer your time to do something on a more philanthropic level. This helps others and lets you feel useful and needed. You may also help the patient indirectly by volunteering for a brain injury-related cause.

Use Lists, Computers, Smartphone APPS, Timers and Post-it Notes

Brain-injured or not, when people are stressed, memory often suffers. Instead of trying to force yourself to remember something. Write everything down. This way you can help clear your head. Take advantage of technology for creating journals, to-do lists, and electronic reminders. You will be amazed at how relieved you will be that you do not have to remember a dozen or more items. Your mind will be more available for more important things, like being mentally and emotionally available for yourself and others.

CHAPTER SIX: FINANCIAL ISSUES

---

*"We used up all our savings and had to sell
our house because we could no longer pay the
monthly mortgage. My wife could not work
full-time because she was my caregiver. It
was when we contacted an attorney and
learned about our options that things turned
around."*

- T.G., Brain-injury Survivor

Families going through this crisis know too well the
financial burden involved in treating and rehabilitating the
patient. What many families are not always prepared for is
how the patient and his family will be taken care of
financially for the long term. Insurance typically covers
costs associated with treatment and rehabilitation, but
families are often at a loss when it comes to planning
income sources for future household and well-being costs.

Some of the sources for both categories of financial assistance are outlined below.

Funding for Rehabilitation

The Patient Protection and Affordable Care Act (aka Obamacare) was signed into law on March 23, 2010; and upheld by a Supreme Court ruling on June 28, 2012. It requires that all Americans have health insurance by 2014 or pay a fee for each month without the minimum essential coverage described in the law. The 10 essential benefits include: ambulatory patient services (outpatient care), emergency services, hospitalization, maternity & newborn care, mental health services & addiction treatment, prescription drugs, rehabilitative & habilitative services and devices, laboratory services, preventative/wellness services & chronic disease treatment and pediatric services.

Private Insurance

Medical costs associated with illness or an accident are covered by private health insurance, either with an individual or group plan. *The insurance must already have been in place at the time of injury.* While the Affordable Care Act protects against being denied coverage for a pre-existing condition, enrollment is limited to the annual enrollment periods unless you have a qualifying life event (examples: moving to a new state, certain changes in income, and changes in your family size (if you marry, divorce, or have a baby). The amount of coverage for each insurance, doctors and hospitals covered, and services covered, will vary among different policies. So it is important to contact the health insurance carrier to find out specific benefits.

Medicare

Medicare is available to individuals during the 7 month period surrounding their 65th birthday (initial enrollment period begins 3 months before turning 65, the month they turn 65, and 3 months after), or who have a disability, or who have chronic kidney disease. It is administered by the federal government, and applied for through the Social Security Administration. Medicare coverage has two parts. Part A covers hospital services including inpatient hospital services, skilled nursing facility care, and home health care. It does not usually require payment. Part B covers physician services, laboratory services, and outpatient hospital care. Supplemental Medicare options are available to fill the Medicare gaps-Medigap, Medicare Advantage (Part C), and Medicare Prescription Drug Coverage (Part D). These are sold by insurance companies approved by Medicare. The Affordable Care Act does NOT replace Medicare but reforms it by extending the rights and benefits to those who qualify.

Medicaid

This is a jointly-funded project between the federal and state governments to assist states in providing medical care to eligible needy individuals. Within broad national guidelines, each state establishes its own set of eligibility criteria, type, duration, amount, and scope of services, and rate of payment. Check with the Medicaid program in your state for details about coverage.

Workers Compensation

If a person is injured while at work, the employer's workers compensation policy can cover much of the services required for treatment. Each policy is different and maintains strict eligibility requirements. These need to be verified with the patient's employer and appropriate state offices. Be sure to find out about pay due to vacation time, sick leave, and short or long-term disability income. Check the possibility of an extended leave of absence being granted, and eligibility for pension benefits. Some insurance policies provide for supplemental income following accidents. Workers' compensation may also provide income in some cases.

Military Coverage

TRICARE provides healthcare for active duty U.S. service members (Army, Navy, Air Force, Marine Corps, Coast Guard, Commissioned Corps of the US Public Health Service and the National Oceanic and Atmospheric Administration), National Guard and Reserve members, retirees, military families, survivors, and others registered in the Defense Enrollment Eligibility Reporting System (DEERS). Registration can be completed at uniformed services identification card-issuing facilities. The benefits and plans vary according to the beneficiary's category. It is critically important for sponsors & beneficiaries to keep their DEERS information current. (*www.tricare.mil*).

The Veterans Health Administration (VA) is the health program for eligible military Veterans. Enrollment satisfies the Affordable Care Act health coverage requirement. Health care services are free for most veterans. Comprehensive medical benefits including preventive, primary, and specialty care; prescriptions; mental health care; home health care; geriatrics and extended care; medical equipment and prosthetics; and more. (*http://explore.va.gov*).

Crime Survivor's Compensation

If the brain-injury resulted from an assault or violent crime, the survivor may be eligible for benefits through this program. Approval for benefits is through an application process initiated by contacting the local justice administrative office.

Victims of violent crimes can also receive some reimbursement for eligible losses from the state when losses cannot be reimbursed from other sources. The California Victim Compensation Board (State Board) administers the program that is primarily funded by restitution fines that courts order convicted offenders to pay in every case. Losses eligible for State Board claims payments include: medical and medical-related expenses for a victim, including dental expenses; funeral and burial expenses for deaths by criminal acts up to $5000, relocation expenses up to $2,000 per household, outpatient mental health treatment or counseling and in-patient psychotherapy costs, for actual victims, wage losses for up to five years following the date of a crime, up to 30-days of wage losses for a parent or legal guardian of a minor victim who has been hospitalized or has died as a result of the crime, support losses for legal dependents of a deceased or injured crime victim, home security systems or improvements up to $1,000 if the crime occurred in victim's home, and crime scene cleanup for up to $1,000 if a victim died as a result of a crime inside a residence http://www.vcgcb.ca.gov/victims/.

Long-Term Sources of Income

Supplemental Security Income (SSI)

SSI is available to disabled individuals (defined according to the Social Security Administration) who have never been employed, have a low income, few assets, or were disabled prior to having contributed to the Social Security fund. Eligibility is based on financial need. SSI benefits are considered a supplement, and the amount paid can vary from state to state. Application is through the Social Security Administration.

Social Security Disability Income (SSDI)

SSDI is available to individuals whose disability occurred within five years of their last employment, and have been employed a specified length of time. Spouses over age 62 may receive benefits, as well as a spouse of any age who is caring for a child who is disabled or under age

16. Widows and widowers over age 50 who become disabled are eligible for this benefit provided their deceased spouse would have met the requisite employment criteria. Unmarried children may also receive benefits, as long as certain criteria are met. There are no financial requirements for this benefit, and benefits can be received until age 65. After age 65, SSDI benefits automatically convert to Social Security retirement benefits. Application is through the Social Security Administration.

CalWorks

What began as *Aid to Families with Dependent Children* became *Temporary Assistance for Needy Families* in 1996. In California, the program is called CalWorks--a welfare program that provides cash and services as short-term assistance for housing, food, clothing, medical care, and utilities. Application is through the local Department of Social Services (http://www.cdss.ca.gov/calworks/) or the local county welfare department.

JOURNEY TO RECOVERY

CHAPTER SEVEN: LEGAL ISSUES

A brain-injury survivor may have several legal issues to consider, including whether or not the injury is the responsibility of another party. It will be helpful for family members to become familiar with some of the laws and acts listed below, as well as others that are not mentioned here.

If you believe that your loved one's injury may be the fault of another, you should seek legal counsel immediately. Do not delay in finding legal representation because there may be time limits – called statutes of limitations – that prohibit you from seeking compensation after a certain amount of time passes. Organizations such as the San Diego Brain Injury Foundation are great resources for helping your find legal counsel that specialize in brain injuries.

Laws Relating to Brain Injury
Personal Injury Law

If an individual has sustained a brain injury as a result of the action or inaction of another person or entity, they may file a personal injury lawsuit against the person or entity responsible to recover monetary damages. Each personal injury case involves establishing liability and damages. Liability refers to demonstrating that the person or entity being charged is legally responsible for the injury. Damages refer to the amount of monetary damages, which depends upon the extent or amount of injury suffered. There are certain time limits (statute of limitations) for filing a legal action and failure to meet the deadline permanently prevents recovery in a court proceeding. In addition, the longer the delay in hiring a lawyer, the staler the evidence becomes, making effective legal action more difficult. If you think your injury may have been the fault of someone else, you should immediately seek legal help.

Medical Malpractice

Medical Malpractice is a form of personal injury and may be handled by a personal injury attorney, but it bears separate discussion. Medical malpractice typically results from negligence or wrongdoing on the part of the physician or other health care provider. This can take the form of surgical error, improper diagnosis, failure to diagnose, medication errors, lack of informed consent, among other matters. Signing a physician's consent form does not give the physician the right to perform at substandard levels.

To claim medical malpractice, the brain injury survivor (victim) must establish the health care provider's (defendant) legal duty, that they failed to meet the standard of reasonable care relating to that duty, resulting in injury to the survivor.

The patient has a legal right to view their own records. It is essential to file a claim as soon as possible, so as to avoid the statute of limitations expiring and causing the case to be dismissed as untimely. Each state has a different statute of limitations, so check with a local personal injury or medical malpractice attorney.

Legislative Acts

Over the past several decades, Congress has passed a number of acts to protect the rights of disabled citizens. If at any time you feel your loved one is being treated unfairly, be sure to contact a governmental agency, attorney, or go online to find out more about his rights. Listed below are brief descriptions of some relevant acts, along with the year they were passed or amended.

Olmstead Act (1999) determined that it is a violation of the Americans with Disabilities Act (ADA) to require disabled individuals to be treated in an institution versus in a community based setting. What this means for the brain-injured patient is that if they want to receive treatment and/or services in the community rather than in a nursing home, for example, they are legally entitled to do so. If the state refuses, then the state is violating the ADA unless it can provide sufficient reason. The Olmstead decision does not, however, give an individual the right to remain in an institution if the state determines that individual should be placed back into the community (www.ADA.gov).

The Fair Housing Act (1968) prohibits discrimination in the sale, rental and financing of dwellings based on race, color, religion, sex or national origin. Title VIII was amended in 1988 to include individuals with disabilities (www.hud.gov/offices/fheo).

The Rehabilitation Act (1973) requires vocational rehabilitation agencies to develop an "individualized written rehabilitation program" for each individual receiving services. Section 504 of the Act provides opportunities for reasonable accommodations for disabled adults and children in education, employment and other settings; and protects disabled individuals from discrimination in federally assisted programs and activities. Sections 501 and 503 protect the disabled from employment discrimination by federal agencies or federal contractors.

The Americans with Disabilities Act (ADA) (1990) prohibits discrimination in employment (for employers of 15 employees or more), public services, public accommodations and services that are operated by private entities, and telecommunications. State and local governments are covered regardless of size (www.ADA.gov).

The Rehabilitation Act Amendments (1992) recognizes that disabled individuals are capable of making informed decisions, are competent, have many abilities, and want to participate in normal routines. Title I presumes that individuals with disabilities, including

64

those with severe disabilities, are capable of engaging in gainful employment. Title VII establishes standards for independent living.

The Ticket to Work and Work Incentives Improvement Act (1999) "Social Security's Ticket to Work Program is a free and voluntary program available to people ages 18 through 64 who are blind or have a disability and who receive Social Security Disability Insurance (SSDI) or Supplemental Security Income (SSI) benefits." The intent is to decrease the reliance on disability payments, offer a disabled person the opportunity to re-enter the workplace and be financially independent of government assistance (http://www.ssa.gov/work/overview.html, 2014).

When seeking legal representation for your brain injury survivor it is vital you find an attorney who has experience handling clients with brain injuries. Attorneys who have worked with other survivors in the past – or who specialize in brain injury cases – will be better able to help you and your family in seeking compensation.

Patient Autonomy Issues

Along with legal and financial considerations, that should be attended to, are issues related to the brain injury survivor's autonomy. Decisions must be made relating to medical treatment, management and use of funds and property, and even designating caregivers for the injured individual's dependent children. Some of these decisions will need to be made immediately, and some over time. We strongly urge you to seek the advice of attorneys specializing in legal, financial, and long-term issues specific to brain-injured individuals and their families.

Guardianship

A guardianship is a legal relationship between the brain injury survivor (ward) and a court-appointed individual (guardian). The guardianship is established once a judge determines that the disabled individual is "incompetent," based on medical documentation. The guardian is given the duty and right to act on behalf of the injured person to make personal, legal, and financial decisions that may affect all aspects of the their life.

Although appointing a guardian can be difficult and emotional for families, it should be determined as soon as possible whether this is the best option. Family members should consult with their attorney, physician, social worker, and proposed guardian for help in making this determination.

Power of Attorney

This is a written legal agreement by which one person (principal) appoints another person (agent) to act on their behalf. The agent is given either restricted or broad authority to make decisions ranging from medical treatment to financial decisions. A power of attorney is similar to a guardianship, except that it typically requires little, if any, court supervision, and is selected by the brain-injured person. The brain-injured individual must be competent enough to select a valid power of attorney, and that selection must be made very carefully, as the court is not closely monitoring the agent. A power of attorney may be executed for specific purposes or more globally.

Conservatorship

This is similar to a guardianship with the exception that the brain-injured individual does not need to be declared incompetent by a judge. The relationship is still established in the court, however. Conservators are primarily responsible for managing the brain-injured person's financial affairs, but may also extend to issues of personal well-being.

Trusts

The use of a trust can be an additional method for managing the property of an individual incapable of managing it on their own. The "trustee" handles the investment and distribution of funds in such a way as to benefit the brain-injured person, and the trustee's conduct is enforceable by law. If trust property requires expert management, a bank or other institution can be named as trustee. Trusts can be designed to be rigid or flexible in how funds are invested and distributed, depending upon the needs of the injured individual.

Estate Planning

Estate planning involves arranging for the management and disposition of an individual's estate following their death. This may include the use of wills, trusts, insurance policies, and other devices. Trusts may be created to ensure adequate financial resources for the injured individual after the death of a family member or caregiver.

CHAPTER EIGHT: BEYOND REHAB

Many people believe that once a brain-injured person has regained basic functioning that they are "recovered"; and no longer needs assistance. While that may be true in the sense of physical or occupational rehabilitation, there are still issues for which the person will need guidance. Even if a brain-injury survivor is capable of living independently, they still has to adjust to a new way of life, a new sense of identity, new relationships, and changes in their job skills or work relationships. This may sound trivial compared to what they previously went through, but these can be huge issues for the survivor.

Practical Issues for the Patient

Here are some typical challenges that brain injury survivors face.

Adjusting to New Realities in Daily Life

Imagine you are a brain-injury survivor and have been labeled as "recovered" by your physician. You may still have problems with your memory, attention span, organization skills, depression and planning. You can't hear very well, and you can't walk without a cane. On a typical day, your alarm goes off, but you don't hear it, so you wake up late. Not only that, but you allotted yourself the same amount of time it used to take you to get ready in the morning, except that now it takes you over twice as long. You can't remember where your socks are. You forgot how to use the toaster, and you forgot to take your medication.

You can no longer drive yourself to work or to run errands so you have to take a bus, but you forgot how to get to the bus stop and even which bus to take. You're getting tired from walking around the neighborhood with a cane looking for the bus stop, and once you get there, people are staring at you because you walk "funny." You forget the names of the people you work with. Perhaps you have been "demoted" to a simpler job. Now it's time to go home and cook dinner, but you can't get yourself organized enough to put a meal together, so you eat some crackers. You have trouble getting your pajamas on, forget to set the alarm, and you can't fall asleep.

For some, this may sound extreme, and for others, this sounds like a "good" day. A brain-injury survivor may have to contend with scenarios just like these, and even though the scenarios will get easier, it may take some time. There may also be some things that will never be the same, such as their memory, organizational skills, and the ability to walk unaided. There will be stares and even comments from strangers, and awkward comments from friends, acquaintances, and family members.

The brain-injury survivor will be seen in a different light by almost everyone around them. Some people may feel pity; others will feel admiration. If the person appears normal physically but has cognitive difficulties, people may even feel annoyed and impatient with his limitations. Hopefully, though, most people will treat the brain injury survivor as the individual they have always been and is now.

Regaining a Sense of Identity

"My life as a husband, a father to my 9-year-old son, an industrial consultant, and fiction writer changed forever. Some aspects for the worse, but some for the better."

- D.M., Brain-injury Survivor

One of the major issues brain-injury survivors often find they can no longer define themselves by their jobs, hobbies, relationships, social status, or possessions. They must find a way to acclimate themselves to their new realities. They learn to focus on what they are able to do now. A father may not be able to help his kids with their homework, but he can now spend more time with them and laugh. He may not be the shrewd businessman he once was, but he has discovered his compassionate side and wants to help others. He can still joke and make people laugh, and this comforts those who remember him for his humor. He cannot dance without a cane, but he tries, and has learned to be more loving with his wife.

The process of regaining a sense of identity will be different for everyone. Some people may want time to figure it out on their own, and others will want plenty of support and guidance from their families. Whatever the method, families should respect the needs and wishes of the survivor.

Reforming Relationships

A woman may identify herself as a wife, mother, sister and supervisor. With the injury comes a change in identity, a change in roles, and a subsequent change in relationships. The relationships may not change for the worse or even end. In fact, many relationships can become stronger and more satisfying.

One of the crucial elements in reforming relationships is forgiveness. If a brain-injury survivor was once cruel and mean-spirited, the injury may have turned them around into a caring and responsible individual. Family members and friends need to be able to forgive the past. There may also be the scenario in which a kind and gentle person has turned into an angry and pessimistic person. Try to forgive that as well. If you know it is not in their "nature," perhaps there is a biological reason for the new behavior that they cannot control. Forgiveness may even need to come without an apology from the injured person, because they may not be aware of any prior or current offensive behaviors.

If a survivor has children, the issue of reforming relationships can be very complicated. Parents have their traditional roles, and children know this. When those roles change, such as when the parent is no longer able to serve as an authority figure, the children may rebel, retreat, or exhibit other harmful behaviors. If this is an issue in your family, we strongly urge you to get family counseling to help work this out.

Work relationships can also prove to be difficult to redefine. Whenever there is a hierarchical relationship that has changed, respect can become a big issue. If a survivor is returning to work in a reduced role, or even in the same role, coworkers and subordinates may not know how to behave appropriately. It may be helpful, on the first day back to work, for the survivor to provide an outline (verbal or written) of their new abilities, what the coworkers can expect, how they would like to be treated, and how they can expect to be treated.

Friendships may fade. At first, some friends will visit often, send cards and flowers, and call to say hi. But as time goes on, these people will carry on with their lives and not think about how difficult life is for someone else. Instead of dwelling on lost friendships, patients and caregivers should encourage formation of new friendships, perhaps with other survivors.

Reforming old relationships is a team effort. The survivor and their family, friends, and coworkers must work together to define and establish each person's new role. These roles should be clearly outlined, agreed upon, respected and flexible.

Being "Productive"

Return to School

Adult brain injury survivors may choose to return to school for vocational retraining, to complete a degree, or simply for personal enrichment. Returning to school can be particularly challenging because of the high, constant demand on the student's ability to learn and recall new information and to effectively organize their time. Institutions of higher learning which receive federal or state funding generally have Disabled Students Service and Programs offices (DSPS), sometimes called Disabled Student Services (DSS) or other similar titles. DSPS offices provide educational support services, specialized instruction, and reasonable accommodations for students with verified disabilities so that they can participate as fully and benefit as equitably from their education as their non-disabled peers. It is advisable that brain injury survivors make use of these services and accommodations. Typically, a Student Educational Contract (SEC) is developed for each student which links their goals, curriculum, and accommodations to their specific disability-related educational limitation. It is the student's responsibility to access the accommodations listed on their SEC.

Examples of reasonable accommodations can include, but are not limited to:

- priority registration,
- specialized counseling/tutoring,

- test proctoring (to allow the student to take the test in a more quiet environment),
- additional time on tests,
- note taking services,
- access to adaptive equipment/software,
- options to record lectures,
- disabled parking, etc.

Some colleges, universities, or continuing education programs may offer specialized courses, such as study skills, etc., for brain injury survivors.

Job Placement and Return to Work

One of the most intimidating aspects of recovery for the brain-injury survivor is the prospect of going back to work. There are many reasons that a survivor may have for returning to work. Not only is it a way to earn money, but it is also a chance to have social contact, structure to the day, and stimulation. During this process, the survivor may want to build up stamina by volunteering, taking a class, and engaging in leisure activities. If the survivor can return to their prior job, some of the suggestions mentioned previously about work relationships can be useful (see p. 75) It may also be helpful for the survivor to meet with their employer beforehand to review the job position, duties, requirements, and behaviors expected of the employee. Any accommodations the employer can provide to assist the survivor should be discussed as well.

Examples of reasonable accommodations can include, but are not limited to:

- Install ramps, handrails, and handicapped parking spaces
- Clear equipment that obstructs pathways
- Provide written job instructions, goals, strategies
- Allow flexible scheduling, including part-time initially, job-sharing, and/or more work breaks, if needed
- Provide additional time to learn (or relearn) duties
- Break tasks and assignments into smaller steps
- Provide picture diagrams of problem-solving techniques (e.g., flow charts)
- Set weekly meetings with the employee to discuss productivity and workplace issues. (*Job Accommodations Network*, 2003)

If the brain-injured individual needs to look for a new place of employment, they should seek assistance from community resources, brain-injury organizations, or job placement agencies. Consulting with your physician and meeting with the Department of Rehabilitation is a good place to start. Volunteering can give the person good feedback on their interests, abilities, and strengths and challenges. It is a good idea for the individual to be truthful about his or her abilities to any prospective employer or placement agency. The individual should ask what the specific duties of any job are, including physical requirements such as lifting, standing for long periods of time, traveling, or anything that may be beyond what the brain-injured individual can do.

The Americans with Disabilities Act (see Chapter Seven) prohibits prospective employers from discriminating against disabled persons. Therefore, being honest about limitations will help ensure the best match between employer and employee. If discrimination appears to be an issue, the person should seek the advice of an attorney. Keep in mind that if a disabled person is not hired because he cannot perform the duties required, it is not considered discrimination.

EMOTIONAL ISSUES FOR FAMILY MEMBERS

"Families also need to grieve the loss of loved ones as they used to be."

- T.M., Brain-injury Survivor

Living with the Patient's New Identity

The person a family once knew no longer exists. They are still living, but perhaps in an altered body and with a different identity. In addition to the range of emotions the family will experience, there may also be a sense of loss. The family may feel grief and may even want to mourn their loss. It may be therapeutic for the family to acknowledge this loss together (with or without the brain injury survivor, depending upon them), to grieve, and even to hold some sort of ceremony. A ceremony may be extreme for some, but by allowing yourselves to feel this loss, you will be able to move on and appreciate the new person in your family.

Once the loss has been dealt with, families can now turn their energy toward accepting their new family member. Many of us would prefer to deny that things are different, but we cannot make any progress if we don't face reality. Get to know the new person in your lives—their likes and dislikes, habits, limitations, abilities, behaviors, and other qualities that make them unique. Learn to accept and appreciate this new person. Realize that this is who they are now, and that it may take time to get used to the new identity.

CHAPTER NINE: BRAIN INJURY DURING CHILDHOOD

"When my son was discharged from the rehabilitation hospital we thought that the worst was behind us. We knew things were different but never did we imagine that after two years our life would be so different from the life we once had. We didn't fully understand that this journey was really just beginning when we left the hospital that day"

-JP, A father of a 5 year old with a brain injury

After a child's brain has been injured, a number of concerns and questions arise.

Will my child live?

If so...when will my child be back to normal?

What are the long-term effects when the brain has been damaged?

Will my child be able to learn?

Will all of my child's abilities return to normal?

What does the future hold for my child?

Will my child be able to go to college and get a job?

Recovery from a brain injury during childhood can be a long and uncertain journey. No two children are alike, just as no two brain injuries are alike. This is because both the brain and the child are still growing and maturing. There can be variability in the symptoms and recovery due to the age at which a child is injured as well as the nature of the brain injury. For example, infants and toddlers with a brain injury may appear "back to normal" within days, weeks or months after the injury. However, as they get older and their brain develops and matures, the parts of the brain that were injured may not function as they should. Depending on the age at which the child's brain injury occurs, the medical professionals can predict the types of cognitive, learning, physical, and emotional challenges that the child may demonstrate now and in the future and develop an appropriate intervention plan to help the child during the recovery process.

Misconceptions about Childhood Brain Injury

There are a few misconceptions about brain injury in children. The first misconception is *"children bounce back from injury more easily than adults do."* Research has shown that the developing brain of a young child is more vulnerable to a brain injury and it may take many years for the consequences of the injury to become evident. For example, a 3-year-old boy who suffers a brain injury may not show problems until he is in school and experiences difficulty learning numbers, letters, and colors. The second misconception is *"physical recovery is a sign that the brain has healed."* Once the child begins to walk after an injury, it is assumed that the child has recovered. However, research has shown that children typically recover their physical ability sooner than cognitive and emotional functions. Learning, memory, behavior and emotional deficits can persist for months and even years.

Common Symptoms after Brain Injury

A brain injury affects physical abilities, thinking skills, emotional and behavioral responses. As with adults, difficulties common to children injury can include some of the following (BIAA, 2007):

Memory:

- Difficulty recalling previously learned information
- Difficulty remembering a series of multi-step directions
- Difficulty understanding and learning new words and concepts
- Difficulty remembering events of the day

Attention and Concentration:

- Easily distracted in busy and noisy situations
- Difficulty staying on topic
- Difficulty completing tasks

Reasoning and Problem-Solving:

- Difficulty organizing and completing long-term projects
- Difficulty sequencing steps necessary to plan an activity
- Difficulty to come up with solutions

Language:

- Talking around a subject or uses imprecise words
- Does not understand the meaning of a conversation when humor, slang, or metaphors of speech are used
- Difficulty finding the correct words to express themselves

Sensorimotor:

- Requires extra time to complete tasks due to slow processing speed
- Difficulty copying information
- Becomes disoriented in crowded places

Behavior and Emotion:

- Says or does socially inappropriate things
- Becomes easily frustrated
- Is unaware of and denies any impairments resulting from the injury.

Physical:

- Fatigue and lack of endurance
- Headaches
- Decreased motor speed and coordination
- Hearing and vision losses

Rehabilitation for Children with Brain Injury

Because every brain injury is different, the child's rehabilitation plan will be tailored to best meet their special and unique needs. Rehabilitation is the process of restoring abilities that have been lost due to the injury. That process can begin in the intensive care unit (ICU) and continue as long as required. Initially, in the ICU, the medical team will work to prevent complications that impede recovery. Once the child is medically stable, they will likely be transferred to an inpatient or outpatient rehabilitation program. The rehabilitation program will work with the child and family to help relearn skills that the child lost while teaching them to use new strategies to do things in a different way to compensate for the difficulties they are experiencing after a brain injury. Pediatric rehabilitation specialists use play-based therapeutic techniques to engage the child's interests in order to build skills. Children learn best through play to focus on mental and physical skills such as understanding and remembering, learning new concepts, expressing themselves, coordinating motor movements, and managing emotions. Play provides repetition and practice critical after a brain injury and necessary for re-developing lost skills. Play is a natural part of a child's and family's life and allows for carryover and generalization of skills in the home environment. It is well recognized that children's outcome is improved when parents are consistent in following through with home intervention programs which allow for repetition needed for mastery of a skill.

The recovery process may happen over a long period of time. As a general rule, most of the natural recovery will occur in the first year after the injury. However, subtle changes can continue to occur for two to five years after the injury. During the rapid stages of recovery, the intensity of rehabilitative therapy will be at its highest. As recovery slows down, the intensity of therapy will also decrease. As long as the child can show ongoing progress, continuing therapy can be justified.

Returning to School after a Brain Injury

After the child returns home from the hospital or rehabilitation facility, returning to school is the next step in the recovery process. The educational and emotional needs of a child with a brain injury are often different than before. They may have difficulty concentrating, poor judgment, impulsivity, memory difficulties, and disorganization. It is essential to plan carefully for the child's return to school. It is vital to be on the lookout for some of these issues and to report them to their medical providers and/or therapists if they become apparent.

A successful reintegration into the school setting involves essential factors such as 1) collaborative and coordinated planning by medical rehabilitation team, family and school personnel to make appropriate decisions for the development of an optimal educational plan; and 2) provision of specific recommendations regarding school-based interventions and accommodations by the rehabilitation team. Before to returning to school, the medical rehabilitation team should collaborate with the family and school personnel in determining whether the child would benefit from an Individualized Education Plan (IEP) or 504 Plan. According to the Individuals with Disabilities Education Act 2004 (IDEA 2004), cognitive and behavioral difficulties associated with a diagnosis of traumatic brain injury (TBI) qualify individuals for an IEP and special education services in public schools. Some children with brain injury may not meet the criteria for an IEP but would benefit from some accommodations within the school setting and would be assisted by the development and implementation of a 504 plan. A 504 Plan refers to Section 504 of the Rehabilitation Act and the Americans with Disabilities Act (ADA), which specifies that no one with a disability can be excluded from participating in federally funded programs or activities, including elementary, secondary or postsecondary schooling. Disability in this context refers to a "physical or mental impairment which substantially limits one or more major life activities". Both the IEP and the 504 Plan are tools that describe what individualized teaching strategies and accommodations will be given to the child to help him or her learn best in the academic environment. Please refer to the *Resource and Reference* sections at the end of the chapter for information on specific teaching strategies for children with brain injury.

Building Your Child's Self-Esteem and Independence After a Brain Injury

It is difficult to watch a child struggle with the physical, emotional, behavioral, learning and/or social changes after a brain injury. *Guided Success* is a strategy that families can use to help build self-esteem and independence (Deaton, 2006):

- Simplify the task if it is too difficult
- Provide enough cues and support so the child is successful
- Minimize failures to prevent depression and low self-esteem
- Use the child's strengths to build confidence and motivation.

It is important to identify supports that the child needs to learn and make progress at home, in school, and in the community (Deaton, 2006):

- Provide an environment that keeps the child safe.
- Give visual cues if needed for independence (i.e., reminder notes for morning routine).
- Offer plenty of opportunities for stimulation as well as rest and relaxation. However, be aware that over stimulation can lead to behavior difficulties.
- Assign chores that fit the child's abilities and hold the child accountable for getting them done. Give them visual reminders of what they need to accomplish.

- Find the school system that provides the right mix of supports and challenges for the child.
- Help the child's friends have fun and know how to help the child when needed.
- Provide activities that everyone can join.
- Find community recreational options that are accessible and enjoyable.
- Help parents of friends understand the child's abilities and when or why they need help.
- Make sure the child has the opportunity to do things for others (choose a gift, fold laundry, make a card for a special occasion) as this develops self-esteem and compassion, builds relationships, and provides practice of skills.
- Find volunteer activities that are suited to the child's abilities and interests.

Helping Families Cope with Long-Term Consequences of a Brain Injury

A child's brain injury not only affects the child but it also affects everyone in the family. Life is not the same for the parents and siblings after the brain injury. While everyone's situation is a bit different, there are some common problems that many family members experience such as less time for each other, feelings of neglect and isolation, financial worries, role changes of family members, problems with communication, and lack of support from other family members and friends. Family members may also experience feelings of anger, guilt, sadness, lost dreams, and fear for the future. You are not alone in what you are feeling.

Families can cope with the long-term consequences of brain injury by taking time for themselves, keeping a regular schedule, getting regular exercise, participating in support groups, maintaining a sense of humor, being more assertive about getting the support they need, and adjusting the various roles and responsibilities within the family. Over time, families report that that they have built a very different but fulfilling life as they have embraced the struggles and challenges and have a sense of pride for what they have endured and accomplished on behalf of the child with a brain injury.

GLOSSARY

Abulia: Absence or inability to exercise will-power or to make decisions. Also, slow reaction, lack of spontaneity, and brief spoken responses.

Acalculia: The inability to perform simple problems of arithmetic.

Acquired Brain Injury (ABI): An injury to the brain occurring after birth that is not hereditary, congenital or degenerative; does not refer to brain injuries induced by birth trauma

ADL: Activities of Daily Living (dressing, bathing, etc.)

Affect: The observable emotional condition of an individual at any given time.

Agnosia: Failure to recognize familiar objects although the sensory mechanism is intact.

Agraphia: Inability to express thoughts in writing.

Alexia: Inability to read.

Ambulate: To walk.

Amnesia: Lack of memory about events occurring during a particular period of time.

Aneurysm: A balloon-like deformity in the wall of a blood vessel. The wall weakens as the balloon grows larger, and may eventually burst, causing a hemorrhage.

Angiography: An x-ray test that uses a special dye and camera to take pictures of the blood flow and the status of blood vessels.

Anomia: Inability to recall names of objects. Persons with this problem often can speak fairly fluently but have to use other words to describe familiar objects.

Anosagnosia: The apparent unawareness of or failure to recognize one's own functional deficit(s).

Anosmia: Loss of the sense of smell.

Anoxia: A lack of oxygen. Brain cells need oxygen to exist. When blood flow to the brain is reduced or when oxygen in the blood is low, brain cells are damaged.

Aphasia: Difficulty expressing or understanding language; can affect a person's ability to speak in grammatically complete sentences and find words, to comprehend spoken language, and/or read or write.

Apraxia: Partial or complete inability to carry out a planned, purposeful sequence of movements, in the absence of paralysis, sensory changes or deficiencies in understanding.

Aspiration: Inhalation of foods, liquids, or secretions into the lungs due to a swallowing impairment.

Astereognosia: Inability to recognize things by touch.

Ataxia: Interruption of smooth muscular movements, characterized by incoordination.

GLOSSARY

Atrophy: A wasting away or decrease in size of a cell, tissue, organ, or part of the body caused by lack of nourishment, inactivity or loss of nerve supply.

Bilateral: Both sides (of the body).

Catheter: A tube for draining urine; "internal": inserted into the bladder (Foley) or "external": over the penis (condom).

Cerebrospinal Fluid (CSF): The liquid which fills the ventricles of the brain and surrounds the brain and spinal cord.

Chronic: Marked by long duration or frequent recurrence.

Circumlocution: Use of other words to describe a specific word or idea which cannot be quickly retrieved; for example, "that thing with lead that you write with" instead of saying "pencil."

Clonus: A sustained series of rhythmic jerks, usually seen in ankles or wrists, caused by the quick stretching of a muscle.

Closed Brain Injury: See "Traumatic Brain Injury"

Cognitive Retraining: Developing or relearning the processes involved in thinking.

Coma: A state of prolonged unconsciousness from which the patient cannot be aroused, even by powerful stimulation.

Compensatory Strategies: Techniques or devices to compensate or make up for the difficulties incurred after a brain injury; for example, using a detailed day planner to compensate for memory problems.

Concussion: The common result of a blow or jerk to the head usually causing an altered mental state, either temporary or prolonged.

Confabulation: Verbalizations about people, places, and events with no basis in reality.

Contracture: Loss of range of motion in a joint due to abnormal shortening of soft tissues.

Contrecoup: Bruising of brain tissue on the side opposite where the blow was struck.

CT Scan/Computerized Tomography: A series of computerized X-rays of the brain at various levels to reveal its structure and possible lesions and bleeding.

Defense and Veterans Head Injury Program (DVHIP):– Program whose goal is to ensure that all military and Department of Veteran's affairs personnel with TBI receive appropriate evaluation and services for their injuries.

Diffuse Axonal Injury (DAI): A shearing injury of large nerve fibers (white matter) in many areas of the brain.

Diplopia: Seeing two images of a single object; double vision.

Dysarthria: Unclear, slurred speech resulting from weakness and/or incoordination of the muscles used to produce speech and sound.

GLOSSARY

Dysphagia: A swallowing disorder characterized by difficulty in moving food from the mouth to the stomach. It may include problems in positioning food in the mouth.

Edema: Collection of fluid in a tissue causing swelling.

Electroencephalogram (EEG): A procedure that uses electrodes on the scalp to record electrical activity of the brain.

Electromyography (EMG): An insertion of needle electrodes into muscles to study the electrical activity of muscle and nerve fibers.

Endotracheal Tube: A tube that serves as an artificial airway and is inserted through the patient's mouth or nose. The tube may connect a respirator to the patient.

Extension: To straighten a joint, such as straightening the leg at the knee.

Extremity: Arm or leg.

FEES: Stands for Fiberoptic Endoscopic Evaluation of Swallowing. The Speech Therapist is able to view the pharyngeal stage of swallowing by using a flexible fiberoptic laryngoscope that is passed through the nose down to the throat. The patient is given a variety of foods and the patient's ability to swallow each food item is recorded and viewed on a TV monitor.

Fine Motor Activities—Complex activities involving the hand, such as writing and manipulating small objects.

Flaccid: Lacking muscle tone; flabby.

93

Flexion: To bend a joint, such as bending your elbow.

Foley Catheter: A tube inserted into the bladder to drain urine, which collects into a plastic bag.

Functional Independence Measure (FIM): a 7 point scale that measures the level of a patient's disability and indicates how much assistance is required for the individual to carry out activities of daily living.

Gait Training: Instruction in walking, with or without equipment; also called ambulation training.

Gastrostomy Tube (G-Tube): A feeding tube passed directly into the stomach from a surgical opening in the abdomen.

Gross Motor Activities: Large movements of body parts, such as those involved in rolling, sitting up and standing.

Halo: A metal ring used for patients with upper spinal cord injuries which is bolted into and surrounds the patient's head, allowing for proper alignment of the neck and spinal column.

Hematoma: The collection of blood in tissues or a space following rupture of a blood vessel.

Hemianopsia: Loss of half the visual field in one or both eyes.

Hemiparesis: Weakness on one side of the body.

Hemiplegia: Paralysis of one side of the body

GLOSSARY

Hydrocephalus: Enlargement of fluid-filled cavities in the brain, not due to brain atrophy.

Hypertonic: Abnormal increase in muscle tone, or tension.

Hypotonic: Abnormal decrease in muscle tone, or relaxation.

Hypoxia: Insufficient oxygen reaching the tissues of the body.

IEP: An individualized education plan for a student found eligible for special education and/or related services that designates the kinds and extent of services that the student needs.

Initiation Problems: Difficulty starting activities without prompting

Incontinent: Inability to control bowel and bladder functions. Many people who are incontinent can become continent with training.

Intracranial Pressure (ICP): Cerebrospinal fluid (CSF) pressure measured from a needle or bolt introduced into the CSF space surrounding the brain.

Intubate: to place a tube through a patient's mouth to the breathing passage.

Jejunostomy Tube (J-Tube): A feeding tube surgically inserted into the small intestine.

Lability: Frequent shifts in emotional state (may manifest as uncontrolled laughing or crying).

95

Magnetic Resonance Imaging (MRI): A diagnostic procedure that uses magnetic fields to create pictures of the brain's soft tissue to reveal changes in structure.

Malingering: To pretend illness or inability in order to avoid duty or work.

Modified Barium Swallow (MBS): Specialized x-ray study in which the patient is observed swallowing substances that can be seen by fluoroscopy (usually liquid barium or foods coated with barium) to evaluate their ability to swallow safely and effectively. This exam, also called a Video Fluoroscopic Swallowing Exam (VFSE), is often performed with a speech-language pathologist present.

Motor Control: Regulation of the timing and contraction of muscles to produce smooth and coordinated body movement.

Motor Planning: Action formulated in the mind before attempting to carry it out.

Muscle Tone: Used in clinical practice to describe the resistance of a muscle to being stretched.

Nasogastric tube (N/G Tube): A tube which is passed through the nostril and into the stomach to carry food directly to the stomach.

Neglect: An attentional disorder, in which the brain does not attend to or recognize the left side of space or body.

Neologism: Nonsense or made-up word used when speaking. The person often does not realize that the word makes no sense.

Neurodegeneration: Damage or death to nerve cells in the brain, often cause by diseases such as Alzheimer's.

Nystagmus: Fast, uncontrollable movement of the eyes.

Open Brain Injury: see "Traumatic Brain Injury"

Orthopedics: The branch of medicine devoted to the study and treatment of the skeletal system, its joints, muscles and associated structures.

Orthosis: Splint or brace designed to improve body function or provide stability.

Paraplegia: Paralysis of the legs (from the waist down).

Paresis: Muscular weakness caused by nerve damage or disease; can be partial or complete paralysis.

Perceptual Motor: Interaction of vision with motor (muscular) activities such as eye-hand coordination, eating, picking up objects, etc.

Perseveration: Uncontrolled, involuntary repetition of speech, motor activity, or thought patterns.

Persistent Vegetative State (PVS): A long-standing condition in which the patient utters no words and does not follow commands or make any response that is meaningful.

Plateau: A temporary or permanent leveling off in the recovery process.

Post Traumatic Amnesia (PTA): A period of hours, weeks or months after an injury during which the patient exhibits a loss of day-to-day memory.

Premorbid: A term to describe the patient's condition before the injury.

Prosthesis: An artificial limb.

Prone: Lying face down.

Quadriparesis: Lack of control of all four limbs of the body resulting from an injury to the brain (See Paresis).

Range of Motion (ROM): The range of movement available in a joint, measured by degrees.

Respirator: (see Ventilator)

Section 504: Part of the Rehabilitation Act of 1973 that requires schools receiving federal funding to provide reasonable accommodations to allow an individual with a disability to participate

Seizure: Uncontrolled electrical activity in the brain, which may produce a physical convulsion, minor physical signs, thought disturbances, unconsciousness, incontinence, or a combination of symptoms. The type of seizure and accompanying symptoms depends on where the abnormal electrical activity takes place in the brain.

Sensorimotor: Refers to all aspects of movement and sensation and the interaction of the two.

Shunt: A tube surgically placed in the ventricles of the brain to relay and deposit excess cerebrospinal fluid into the abdominal cavity or heart to prevent build-up of fluid and thereby pressure in the brain.

Somatosensory: Sensory activity having its origin elsewhere than in the sense organs (such as eyes and ears); conveys information to the brain about the body and its immediate environment.

Spasm: A sudden, abnormal, involuntary muscular contraction.

Spasticity: A marked involuntary increase in muscle tone (tension) characterized by hyperactive reflex and shortening of the muscle.

Special Education: Specialized teaching & instructional supports to serve students with special educational needs.

Splint: A metal, plaster or plastic support used to position one or more joints properly to reduce muscle tension, increase range of motion and/or allow greater use of the body part.

Strabismus: "Crossed eyes"; eyes are not properly aligned with each other; usually resulting in double vision.

Subdural: Beneath the dura (tough membrane) covering the brain and spinal cord.

Supine: Lying on one's back.

Synergy: Combined action of two or more muscles to form an abnormal pattern of movement. The person cannot move one without the other.

Tactile Defensiveness: Being overly sensitive to touch; withdrawing, crying, yelling or striking when one is touched.

Tracheostomy (Trach): A surgical opening at the front of the throat providing access the trachea or windpipe.

Traumatic Brain Injury (TBI): A non-degenerative, non-congenital insult to the brain from an external mechanical force, possibly leading to permanent or temporary impairment of cognitive, physical, and psychosocial functions. Closed TBIs, in which the skull remains intact, can occur as a result of motor vehicle accidents or falls, blows to the head, or vibration of brain tissue due to explosions, etc., Open TBIs are the result of brain tissue being penetrated by bullets, knives, shattered pieces of skull, etc. Consciousness may be altered or diminished in TBI.

Tremor: Rhythmical movements of a body part that become intensified the harder one tries to control them.

Tremor (Resting): Rhythmical movements while at rest; may diminish during voluntary movement.

Vegetative State: An absence of responsiveness and awareness due to overwhelming dysfunction of the cerebral hemispheres, which higher level thinking and consciousness takes place. Autonomic and motor reflexes and sleep-wake cycles are preserved due to sufficient functioning of more primitive parts of the brain. After four weeks in a **vegetative state** (VS), the patient is classified as in a **persistent vegetative state.** This diagnosis is re- classified as a **permanent vegetative state** (PVS) after about one year following a TBI.

Ventilator: Machine that does the breathing for the unresponsive patient by delivering air with the right amount of oxygen at the right rate.

Verbal Apraxia: Impaired control of proper sequencing of muscles used in speech (tongue, lips, jaw muscles, vocal cords).

Vestibular: Pertaining to the vestibular system in the middle ear and the brain which senses movements of the head. Vestibular disorders can lead to dizziness, poor muscle tone in head and neck, and inability to detect quick movements of the head.

Void: To urinate.

(Glossary references: *Brain-injury Glossary,* HDI Publishers, 1996; Long Island Head Injury Association and *The Essential Brain Injury Guide – Edition 4.0*, 2009, Brain Injury Association of America)

REFERENCES

Brain Injury Association of America, (www.biausa.org) (2014)

Brain Injury Association of America (2007). The Essential Brain Injury Guide: Edition 4.0. Vienna, VA: BIAA.

Betty Clooney Foundation, *Head Injury Fact Sheet, 2003.*Center for Disease Control and Prevention (CDC) (http://www.cdc.gov/traumaticbraininjury/get_the_fact s.html). (2014)Deaton, A. (2006). Helping Children Succeed after Brain Injury. Wake Forest, NC: Lash Publishing.

DePompei, R & Tyler, J (2004). *Learning and Cognitive Challenges: Developing Educational Programs for Students with Brain Injuries.* Wake Forest, NC: Lash Publishing.

Dise-Lewis, J et al. (2002). *Brain Injury: Strategies for Teams and Re-education for Students.* Denver, CO: BrainSTARS Program.

Job Accommodations Network (JAN), (http://askjan.org/media/Brain Injury.html#acc, updated March, 2013.

National Association of State Head Injury Administrators, www.nashia.org, *June 2003*

National Institute of Health: National Institute of Neurological Disorders and Stroke, www.ninds.nih.gov, *June 2003*

Schoenbrodt, L. (Ed) (2001). *Children with Traumatic Brain Injury: AParents' Guide.* Bethesda, MD: Woodbine House.

Sellers, CW & Vegter, CH. (2000). The Young Child: *Myths & facts about brain injury in infants, toddlers & preschoolers.* Wake Forest, NC: Lash Publishing.

Online Resources:

Brainlinekids

- *http://www.brainline.org/landing_pages/features/blkids. htmlry-a-parents-guide-_pageall.html*

Brain Injury Association of America

- *http://www.biausa.org/brain-injury-children.htm*

Brain Injury Guide and Resources

- *http://braininjuryeducation.org/*

CBIRT: The Center on Brain Injury Research & Training

- *http://cbirt.org/*

Lash & Associates Publishing/Training, Inc.

- *http://www.lapublishing.com/*

LEARNet (Brain Injury Association of New York State)

- *http://projectlearnet.org/project_learn.html*

Project BRAIN

- *http://www.tndisability.org/article/project-brain*

San Diego Brain Injury Foundation

- *http://sdbif.org/*

Made in the USA
San Bernardino, CA
14 September 2016